from

f + R

xx

*For my* *Nan*

*For my* Nan

FOR MY NAN

© WPL 2006

Text by Howard Baker, Edna Beach, Shirley Collins, Anne Dodds, A. Fisher,
Elaine Ford, Gail Hirst

Edited by J. Rose Barber
Design by WPL

Printed in China
Published by WPL 2006

ISBN 1-904264-46-8

WPL
The Perfume Factory
140 Wales Farm Road
London  W3 6UG
Tel: +44 (0) 208 993 7268
Fax: +44 (0) 208 993 8041
email: info@wpl.eu.com
www.wpl.eu.com

Nan, this book's for you
as I just want to say
all the things that go unsaid
as life goes on each day.

If I think about the reasons why
you mean so much to me,

it's hard to know just where to start,
as there are such a lot you see !

From my earliest memories
you were always there,
and I've never ever doubted
just how much you care.

I really do appreciate
all the things you do,
and the kind and helpful way you have
of simply being you.

You've always been so patient,
  so gentle and so kind,

you're there when I need you
and never seem to mind.

No matter what, you try and make
    lots of time for me,
I always feel so welcome
        and as special as can be.

Of all the people in my life

   you've always been someone

who's shown a real interest
   in the things that I have done.

My world is just a happier place
knowing that you care,
and when I need someone to talk to
I know you're always there.

You're such a special person
with qualities so rare,
compassion, understanding
and a warmth beyond compare.

You're full of optimism,
generosity and grace,
and if everyone had a Nan like you
the world would be a happier place.

The values I have
learnt from you
will always
see me through.

They have shaped my character –
who I am and what I do.

Thank you very much, Nan,
for so much love and care,

and for all the
wonderful memories
that you and I can share.

The years between us fade away
whenever we're together

and the happy times we've had
will be with me forever.

We have a special bond
that distance can't erase

and I always feel my spirits lift
when I see your smiling face.

The times we spend together
mean so much to me,
we get along so well
and I enjoy your company.

You really are someone
on who I can depend

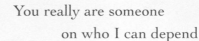

and as well as being a lovely Nan,
you also are my friend.

Putting others first
comes naturally to you,
you have the warmest heart
and it shows in all you do.

You have been there for me,
all throughout my life,

listening, understanding

    and giving good advice.

You're always happy for me
    when things are going great
and also standing by
    to help me celebrate.

You are a special Nan
and a good confidante too.

I know whatever happens

I can rely on you.

I hope you know
    beyond all doubt
how very much I care,

and how grateful
I have always felt
    just knowing you are there.

I count myself as lucky
for I could travel far,
and never find myself a Nan
who's as lovely as you are.

You know how to make me smile
        and the kind things that you do
make me feel so very glad
        that I have a Nan like you.

If I was told that I could choose
from all the Nans there are,

there is no doubt I'd pick you out,

because, Nan, you're a star !

You're a very precious Nan
of whom I'm very proud,
a special type of person
who stands out from the crowd.

I can't think of anyone
        in this whole world, it's true,

who deserves the best that life can bring

quite as much as you.

You're an absolute treasure
and I hope you can see,
you're a wonderful Nan
who means so much to me.

Whether we're together
or many miles apart,

you are always with me
forever in my heart.

Now you've read this book
I really hope you know,

although I rarely say it, Nan,

I will always love you so.